I Licked A Slag's Deodorant

Jim Cartwright

I Licked a Slag's Deodorant was originally produced at The Royal Court Theatre Upstairs on 27 November 1996. The cast was as follows:

Man Tim Potter
Slag Polly Hemingway

Director Jim Cartwright
Designer William Dudley
Lighting Designer Simon Corder
Sound Designer Paul Arditti

Characters

Man
Slag

The Time
Now

Place
A corner of London

Act One

Lights up on a **Man** *on corner of a bed, in spotlight, only corner of bed can be seen. Rest of stage in total blackness. He is in trousers and vest. He sits for thirty seconds.*

Man   The carpet was damp. I was cold in my vest. I licked her deodorant while she was out the room, what's happening to me? There was a bucket under the sink and a bottle of beer. She never came back. She must have took the money and run. I sat there until it went dark. It was no use. I picked up the deodorant from among her things: a brushful of hairs, a plastic earring, a contraceptive in a packet, like a silver cockroach. I put the deodorant in my pocket. I didn't take the bottle of beer. It could have been up someone's backside for all I knew. I went home. I had licked a slag's deodorant.

Blackout.

Lights up.

He is against a brick wall. Holding his face. Talking through his hands.

Man   It was pitch black outside. I walked fast. I bumped into an old man outside a pub. He stumbled. Someone shouted 'He was trying to do Juiee-Jitsu on Stan.' Someone shouted 'Cut him.' The old man said 'Kick him as hard as you can in the face, that'll do me.' A Fatman threw me to the ground. I saw my blood running silver, in the moonlight, a slow silver cockroach crawl. I won't never go back there again. It took me a long time to get home all the street lamps looked swollen. I won't go back there again. I've better things to do.

Blackout.

Lights up.

He is sitting. Telly on with sound, but low. Light of it flickering over his face. Eating fish-fingers and beans as best he can, with sore face.

Man (*loud over the telly noise*)   On the way up, I saw them bring down a man I knew, on a stretcher. They found him dead in his flat, covered in dust and beetles. I wondered where he'd got to. When we passed on the stairs, usually he'd crack a joke. I knew there was no chance of one tonight, but I still hung on like I always did, until he'd passed. They don't know if someone killed him or he killed himself or someone killed him or he died. I don't know how they expect you to manage alone. It's hard even for me, and my mum showed me how to cook and wash me knackers. And what would she say now of her one and only, who licked a slag's deodorant.

Blackout.

Lights up.

He is standing in pub. Glass of beer in hand.

Man   I'm drinking fast tonight. My right eye's still shaking from the Fatman's kick and the beer feels like it's going in crooked. A stripper will come on soon. I'll watch from here. In this place they don't get rowdy when they strip, but quiet. Like they're examining her. I don't know what come over me at the slag's. I live alone. I watch young women on the adverts. I see them in the paper. I have an old magazine under the lino. And sometimes, in bed at night sexy feelings comes on me like a coat I can't take off. Is it that, that drove me to her, that lay my tongue so low.

Strip music starts up. He watches blank. Coloured lights play over his face. A bra hits him in the face, he puts it in his pocket.

Blackout.

Lights up on brick wall.

Man (*drunk*)   A toast to me friend, the joker on the stairs. It was the way he told 'em. I liked him because he was sadder than me. Because behind the jokes he knew how the loneliness falls and falls and falls. Anyone could see he was ill. He was thin. He wore the same clothes. There was something of the diarrhoea about him. Brown suit, brown tie on dirty shirt. We stopped on the stairs. He told his joke. I can still hear it echoing, empty men's laughter, off stone.

Blackout.

Lights up.

He is in a disco, flashing lights all over him. Hip-hop music. He stands for thirty seconds.

Blackout.

Lights up on him on a bar-stool. Still in disco but music in distance.

Man   I didn't believe it. I saw the slag. First of all I was afraid, I thought she was going to come over and say was it you who licked my deodorant. But she didn't even recognise me. Then I wanted to go over and say something. Give her a piece of my mind. Let her know once and for all I'm never going back there again. I've better things to do.

Takes drink. Walks in her direction.

Blackout.

Lights up.

The **Slag***'s room.*

Same cover on bed. He is sitting on the corner of bed. Still in suit, tie down, staring.

Man   She took me back to her place, again.

She left me.

Pause.

Again.

Thirty seconds pass.

He slowly takes out the stripper's bra from his coat pocket. From the other coat pocket he takes out the deodorant. He carefully coats the inside of the bra with the deodorant. Then he puts the bra up to his eyes and face and straps and fastens it round.

Sits in suit and with bra round his face, crying, and crying and crying.

Slag *against brick wall.*

Slag   I left him.
Again, I took his money. Twice in one night. The soft twat.
I have no worries, I know he'll go quietly. How long could
anyone stay in that room? The smell. The wallpaper,
thousands of tiny twat pink roses fading to spit. The ceiling
like the surface of spunk moon. The carpet like an Indian
takeaway. It's always in my head. All thoughts have to pass
in or out of it, even sleep. Only thing will break it into tiny
pink rose pieces of eight is the shattering white of my Uncle,
Dr Crack.

She steps out of the light.

Business sir?
£20 sex.
£15 oral.
£10 hand relief.

Blackout.

Man *still on bed. Bra around his face. Breathing difficult and noisy. He speaks.*

Man   My mother cared I think. My shirt was always
tucked in. She gave me Swiss roll in front of the telly. My
father was a drinking man and he went. We lived in an old
flat. Distempered walls. Ancient war lavy and chain, I
sometimes dream I am pulling that chain. Were there
windows? There must have been.

Blackout.

Lights up.

Slag *is on a pub chair. Drink in hand.*

Slag   I could do with a toot now but I can't find the
Fatman, he's not in the pub. He's not in the curry house. I
know I'm dripping cold sweat and my eyes are heading
inward. But really, once on my back, who looks as the fucks
are shovelled in. Fatman where are you if you're not eating
and drinking! Fatman! There's work everywhere for the
enterprising, I've just made a tenner under the table here,
with a hand shandy. He sat looking at me like he was
playing the fruit machine. Some people stare at me in here
and they know what I do. Some don't. You feel a bit
famous.

Blackout.

Lights up.

Man *still bra round face.*

Man   At school I did never fit. Only time I was noticed
was the time I wet myself in assembly. After that I had to
stay in the classroom with the Jehovah's Witnesses.
Playtime, everything ran round me, I stayed still. Life keeps
going by like that, fast faces, here there, round and round
me. Our flat was damp. We never moved. We kept
ourselves to ourselves. We had the occasional visitor. We
had a relative. Uncle Cigburns. We had two records, one of
Kathy Kirby, one of a brass band. But we had the telly.
That's where we'd sit, in its glow, the two of us, texture like
an oil painting. I could touch the light and the dark, run my
fingers through it.

Blackout.

Slag *against brick wall again.*

Slag   I meet men, nobody meets more but I'm lonely like
a dying spunk up a cunt. I never talk to women. After work
I leave the Fuck factory and I go home. My Uncle Crack
climbs on my back.

She passes out of light, to approach a punter.

Fuck £15.

Nosh £10.
Wank and feel around £5.

I've got a place.

She steps back into light.

Fuck you then. Perhaps he got too close and there was my skin.

Blackout.

Lights up.

Man *still on bed, still bra around face.*

Man   My first suit was second-hand. Half-mast, well pressed by Mum. I wore it to Uncle Cigburn's funeral. He left Mum twenty quid. We had a fish and chip supper. She gave me a fiver and I bought a Hot Hits record and some Brut, fuck knows why I never went out. I may have thought the girls would have come to my house to sniff it. I may have put it on when I stood in front of the mirror with Hot Hits playing, in my vest and underpants, imagining.

Blackout.

Lights up.

She is still against the wall.

Slag   I found Fat. But now he's teasing me. He said wait and he'd come back but sometimes he don't come back. He said to me, you can have, but you've got to pay and you have to let me and old Stan shag you. I said whatever. At one time he'd take me when he wanted me, now he hardly does. Thank God. He has a horrible cock, bluey and knobbly, like the shiny joint of a chicken leg bone, like a jabbing, jabbing elbow.

FATMAN! FATMAN!

He can have any of us whores, any way, kiss-me-quick cunts in a row. He's got flats and lock-ups full of stuff, still in boxes. Money hangs from his arse. He says he hates junkies they give everything too easy, they make life so soft it's shit. To spice things up a bit he goes hunting with his pack of man dogs. He caught that poor bastard there tonight, outside the pub, I saw. He threw him down, his head come up like a poptart, he kicked it to fucking jam.

Blackout.

Man *still on bed. Bra on face. Breathing harder.*

Man She left me one Saturday afternoon. I didn't know, I thought she was having a lie-in. I went up after the wrestling. I touched her, she was cold. I still have the chill in my finger. (*Stops.*) Afterwards I got as I wouldn't go out. Stopped cleaning. Shaving. Everything. Lived off fish-fingers. I got so full of them, I could feel the batter going round in my bowels like gravel, the dead fish stacked against my sunken bones. The wall stared at me, I stared back, but neither of us started anything. After the hospital they moved me. They said it took five men to empty the newspapers out the old flat. And a day for them to reach the kitchen floor. My flat now, I never put anything in, never take anything out. Armchair, check. Bed, check. Telly, check. Two-ring cooker and grill, check. Formica table, check. One chair, check.

Blackout.

She is still against wall.

Slag The pubs are closing there'll be a rush soon. I'll lie back and blast off for spunk moon.

FATMAN! FATMAN!

Up they will come, the men of our realm. Snobs who fuck like they're cutting up a fish. Drunks who shag the half inch between your cunt and your bum and never know. Slow lads who look and look. Businessmen who want to go to the loo on you.

(*Sung desperately to the tune of 'Batman'.*) FATMAN! FATMAN! FATMAN! FATMAN!

Fingers, hands, fists, beerbottles, they'd shove fire up if they could, they've lynched my cunt. It hangs like material. You can do with it what you like, I won't feel a thing, I always say yes to everything.

(*Sung more desperately to 'Batman'.*) FATMAN! FATMAN! FATMAN! FATMAN!

Dear Uncle Crack. I want you soothingly sucking my brain. I want your kiss of sugar dancing off the vein. I want your breeze rushing through. Let that crack be sharp. A shot. Shattering the walls, pink rose. Take the street. Fold me up and up in your razored stars. Deliver me from evil. Be my friend.

FATMAN!!!

Blackout.

Lights up.

Man *still on bed.*

Man   I see him now, my joker friend, in the corner of his kitchen scrunched. His coat and suit still on or in his shirt and trousers, one shoe off. And the kitchen floor's dirty and his cheek's stuck to it and there's a bucket under the sink, and there's a bottle of bleach and there's no one, and the telly's playing for days and days and through the night in the dark it's a lantern show rolling over his dead back, one programme after another, then going round again and again, and he's just the same, dead in the corner, or is it me!

Blackout.

Lights up on **Slag**.

Slag   They came back. They followed me up the stairs. Old Stan's head was nearly up my skirt. When we got in the room. I couldn't believe it, the man was still there, but fucking completely bra-faced. He was suffocating I think. Spit bubbles was all coming over the bra. You could stink deodorant and see it like lava on his cheek. I suppose you'd expect me to scream but I just looked. I suppose someone should have given him the kiss of life but the Fatman just slashed him one and blood greased into the deodorant fast as light. He sort of whined but so quiet it was a million miles away.

I wanted him out.

The Fatman said he'd send someone up. We come down. They went somewhere. I went back to the wall.

Blackout.

Lights up on **Man**, *bra still around his face, slashed now, blood coming through.*

He is singing and humming in pain, a Kathy Kirby song.

Lights up on **Slag** *at same time.*

She is against brick wall, maniacally dancing, dancing it seems to the tune.

Then the actual song is played over the scene and into blackout.

Act Two

Wall. **Man** *is lying at the bottom of it. Bloody and beaten, a bucket over his head. The* **Slag** *wanders on, high as a kite now.*

Slag (*to herself / audience*)   A whore high on crack, look up my bum, what do you see? High energy.

Looks.

I recognise that bucket.

Takes it off his head.

No good now.

Tips it up, bra falls out on to floor, blood and deodorant in it. She sees **Man**. *His eyes closed, as though they are stinging, painful. Dried blood on him.*

Slag   Oh, it's you again. This be the third time we met did you know? Maybe that makes us friends. Maybe that makes us family. Come here.

She gets him up.

Stand there now.

She puts him against the wall.

Stand there.

He slides down.

Oh. Oh you.

She picks him up, puts him against wall, turns round front, supports him with her bottom.

By the way what's your name? (*No reply.*)
Ummm. To me, no one ever says their name, or they lie. I do too, my name's been a hundred. Andorra, Perdi, Kissy. Their names: Joe. Ted. Bert. Mr Cavendish. They lie, I always say what's your name, they lie. Later, they call me:

Fuck. Bitch. Cunt darling. But you 'three timer'. You can
call me my real name –
You can call me . . .?
You can call me . . .?
You can call me . . .?
What the fuck is it?
I'm trying to remember. My mother's mouth, what did she
say? My dad he was there. Mum was there. There they are
the two solid bastards of the earth.

What happened next? I came to the city. A man took me
and showed me with his hands. Money did not change
hands, I did. He did fraud on me. Did he name me?

She turns to direct the question to **Man**. *He slips down wall, she
catches him, props him up, holds him with one hand, looking at him.*

By the way do you, do you, by any chance
happen to know the Fatman?

*She turns away from him and again supports him with her bottom and
back.*

You should see the Fatman, you should see the Fatman,
little crack lads, they come to him like refugees of the
nineties, he's fucking Fagin with a gun. You should see the
Fatman. All fat stuff, face fatted out with fat, thigh neck,
belly coming out of a brown T-shirt. You should see, you
should see what I dream, a hundred addicts on him, Moby
Dick style, clawing him, fuck me we're eating him, he's
rising and falling like a great white whale, up then down,
taking us with him, till we rip right through to his heart, a
white flint of crack with a fleck of blood on it. He says he
hates junkies, he hates slags, he hates the bleeding hands
that feed him, he likes (*She puts her fists up in an old-fashioned
boxing guard and rolls them.*) scientific fistics on a Friday night,
he punch hunts (*She punches the air. She turns to him, tenderly.*),
he hit you my darling. Come on we'll go back to your place.

*She links his arm as they are about to set off, glances to one side, then
does a double take, she has seen a potential customer.*

Hey, hey, business.

She walks out the light into the darkness. He collapses down the wall, ends legs splayed, sitting up.

Behind the wall, hear her making it with the 'pick-up'.

In front **Man** *starts singing Kathy Kirby songs.*

●**Slag**   Pay first. You pay first here mate. Get it out. Put one on if you want. It's more if you don't.
Come on then, come on.
Okay, I'll suck it, I'll suck it, give it here, make your fucking mind up.
(*With her mouth full.*) Don't push my head. Don't push my head.
(*With mouth clear.*) Don't push my head.
Right.
No, let me turn round.
Go on. Go on. Get it in then. That's it. It's in.
Fuck me. Go on, fuck me. Fuck me. Go on. Yes. Yes.
You're out again! Here let me do it, it's quicker. Keep fucking still. Come on. Come on. Uh. Uh. Uh. Uh. Uh. Uh. Uh. Uh uh nearly there now uh uh uh. Right uh uh uh. That's it. (*It's over.*)
Right.

She has a coughing fit.

Man *in front still singing Kathy Kirby songs.*

The **Slag** *comes back. She spits.*

Slag   That's the spit o' the whore.

She takes his hand and arm.

Disco, then your place.

She swings him up.

Blackout.

Lights up.

They are in disco, lights flashing, smoke, rave music playing. She is spinning him round and round and round, then lets go, he hits mirror at back.

She carries on dancing. She grabs him from mirror, dances with him, then throws him across floor into a chair. She dances into mirror looking at her reflection. She pulls a lipstick out of her pocket and writes across mirror 'What's my name?'

She turns to face **Man**, *dances, then goes and picks him up by the scruff of the neck and dances him out the disco.*

Blackout.

Lights up.

The **Man***'s place.*

She lowers **Man** *into armchair.*

Slag   Sit yourself down.
I'm off for a look around, have you anything under the bed?
I'm a bit skinned you see. I'll perform sex on you if you like.
I'll look around somewhere in the dark, there must be
something.

She suddenly walks very fast to front of stage.

Walks back. Then goes off.

(*From offstage.*) How's about this fluff under the bed, it's like a
vacuum cleaner bag. It's like putting your head in a vacuum
cleaner bag. You've got the television page with a chip on it.
There's a tin-opener. There's drawers with an old woman's
coat bunched in it. There's a tin with one cooked tomato in
it, and on that tomato is green. There's a case with some
pipes in it. A gum boot. What's this under the lino? a cunt
book. Your clothes are all thick and dark and jammed in.
Not worth going through. HAVE YOU NO BISCUIT TIN
with money in it? HAVE YOU NO STASH? What's under
the sink? a bucket.

Nothing even worth nicking.

Comes back on.

Nothing even worth nicking.
I'm not letting you stay here, come on.

Blackout.

Lights up.

The dark space.

Nothing around them but dark. She holding him up. The sound of a train passing overhead, very loud, till it's gone. The sound of water dripping, the sound of the wind.

Slag   This is a big commitment we're making, do you lawfully matrimise me.
I don't expect much, just don't fucking play around.
(*She looks around.*) The two of us in the dark space.

She pulls her top out a bit.

Look at my bra.

He has a long long look. She puts top back.

(*To audience.*) Look at us. You don't know how dark it's got, I do.

She lets out a scream.

I don't need psychotherapy to find my causes. I see them every night. Bang up to the hooter and boot up the heart base, and one up the jacksy.
And besides them, every night all men come lie on me – fullweight. Kinky Chinks taking ages to come. Glum Northerners with their flat-cap fucks. Jumping Jews like crackerjacks. Slow old darkies, like Bourneville plain. The fucking thick Irish. The fucking thick Welsh. The horrible biting cockney, and all the time, all the time, Pakis. I'm not prejudice in any way, I hate every man jack the same. All get equal measure.
Hang on my mind's gone.

Pause.

Back again.

I forget to mention the MPs and the pickled judges and all the little liars. I forget to mention the vicars wanting a wank, cocks that are there suddenly, a mushroom in the dark with you. I don't like the religious ones, too much greed in the fingers, they have your body like a finger buffet. They are also pork. They are also big underpants.

Pause.

She walks to the front of the stage leaving **Man**. *He slowly begins collapsing.*

(*To audience.*) Do I take it up the shitter? YES.

She walks back. She's in time to catch him before he is completely on floor.

Pause.

(*Holding him and holding her head in her hand.*) It's back! The carpet, the ceiling, the twating roses, the wallpaper is behind my eyes, my eyeball lives on the wallpaper. The pattern is about to cut, the corners are right now peeling up sharp. I can't go back there. I can't go back! (*Hands in her hair, desperate.*) Wait I'm not alone no more. (*Looks at him.*) Thanky. See, I have to have Uncle there see, and Uncle's wearing off. Uncle thwacks me whack an' whack, then goes. Though he has of course his cunning drain, which he keeps from him to me, me to him, always an echo down it, or an itch, or a slug, or a chomping rat, or of a morning an electric wire with the live end jumping all over the place, all through your body, all through your weeping jelly.

Pause.

HANG ON MY MIND'S GONE.

Pause.

Hang on my mind's gone.

Pause.

Back again.

Let us leave this dark.

Blackout.

Lights up.

The **Slag***'s place.*

She has him in a fireman's lift, puts his feet on the ground and lets him roll back on to the bed.

Slag   Now really you should carry me over the threshold, not the other way. Right, right. Settle down on the sprung bung bed and watch.

She sits him down.

She does a little dance.

I could do sex on you if you like. What's next? The carpet's a genuine Fred Bear, but the corners are soaked. I have a wash in them sometimes. Listen, what's that a cockroach? what's that a mouse? this is your only music I'm afraid. And the sound of the walls a-sighing. Now I must prepare. Sing while I do, come on, else I'll kick your fucking arse through your mouth, then ram your head up it fucking fine style, cunt.

She punches him in the eye.

Then loves him better.

Our first tiff. (*She walks away.*) It's always nice when you make up.

Sing to me, go on. (*He sings Kathy Kirby songs.*)
I'll get ready for work.

He sings on.

She prepares to go out, we see her making up, straightening her clothes, rolling on deodorant, she offers it out to him, he stops singing and licks it. Starts singing again.

She finishes, he stops singing.

I'm running away.

He starts to whimper.

Not really. You've got used to me haven't you.

I may have to bring some back, some will be behind the wall, some will be on the run, some I will bring back, some might even call.

See you.

Blackout.

Lights up.

Man *now lives under the bed.*

Man   I now live under the bed. It's fluff balls, it's lots, condoms, squelch, a dry deodorant rolling, other creatures. We're company. Above is whore's bed heaven. I keep just about as still and quiet as I can and do my best. She smokes and snorts and the bits float under the bed. Sugar flying, sugar flying, through the fluff and up my nose. When you're under the bed with Uncle and you can't move, your mind must take it. You're in a solid block, but all your particles are jumping. Sometimes the springs above are a grill. Sometimes sugar-frosted. Sometimes I'm cold. In a trance among the fluff. When the mattress is bouncing and nearly in my face, I think well at least we're company. We talk like sailors in bunks, sharing secrets, she calls her clitoris Knotty Ash. She has her soft side, she has her hard side, she pokes me and I sing to her, Kathy Kirby. As a teenager I always had clothes on, clothes on, things tucked into things. Thick elastic. Vests. Vest, T-shirt, then shirt then woollen jumper, then anorak. Everyone else was walking round like butterflies. I was always in brown, brown or maroon, then sometimes for no reason a bright yellow jumper under the brown. Mother dressed me. The nearest I got to a woman, I scrubbed her back with a loofah. Oh the white skin on the bone, oh the white skin on the bone. It moved like a carrier bag would over a frozen chicken. If I cry, I know it will be her bathwater grey. I have found my rusty spring niche. I know life now, I know it every time a full condom hits my face.

And I take the snowflakes up my nose that flutter down.

She pokes me and I sing to her.

I hear it all.

End.

Production Notes

In the Royal Court production the reverse of the brick wall was mirror and spun round in the blackout for the disco scenes.

The floor was covered with wet black carpet which served for the wet street outside and damp carpet inside. For some of the street scenes the lights of the night (street lights, coloured lights, etc.) were reflected off the wet.

In the Royal Court production it was decided to make the Slag Northern and to alter the line on page 11 to:

Slag   . . . There they are the two solid Barnsley Bastards of the earth.
What happened next? I came down to the city . . .